Recollections of a 1980's British Rail, Southern Region, Train Guard.

By

Clive Bowd.

Dedication.

This short work is dedicated to the staff with whom I worked and the passengers I served, the former for their friendship and camaraderie on the whole, the latter for their understanding and good nature most of the time.

Contents.

Other books available on Kindle by the same author.

<u>Our Black & White Heritage. The part that black and white photography has played in the first half of the twentieth century.</u>

ASIN: B01OG3QNYW.

<u>Tales of The Ridgeway.</u>

A personal exploration of The Ridgeway, its archaeology and history, from Goring-on-Thames to the area around Avebury in Wiltshire.

ASIN: B00YP5YLV.

<u>Morgana's Gold.</u>

An historical action novel set in Arthurian Britain, the tale of a quest and coming of age.

ASIN: B014HCFZ43.

Introduction.

As the train worked its way slowly up the incline out of Ham Street station heading for Rye I settled back in my seat and prepared to write up my log, the guard's van empty of contents other than myself. Cresting the slope, the driver sounded the locomotive's horn giving prior warning to the gatekeeper at Warehorne Crossing that we were just minutes off. Nothing unusual in that, except on this occasion the driver repeatedly sounded the horn. That aroused my curiosity so I got to my feet, went over to the door and let the window down. As I stuck my head out and took in the scene, the realisation dawned that things were not right.

From my position I could see that the crossing gates were closed to us, a car drove over the line, even a pedestrian walked across. My thoughts turned to my training and route knowledge, the former telling me to get on the intercom to the driver, the latter that we didn't stand a chance of coming to a stop short of the gates! It was a decisive moment, not only at the time, but in my career as a train guard.

At this point I feel I should set the background to the events that were about to unfold, that means looking at how I came to be there, not just that day but, in the service of British Rail, Southern Region, as it was at the time. I had been working for several years prior to entering the rail service as management in the retail jewellery business.

Whilst my former career was interesting, even stimulating at times, it failed to pay me enough to maintain a wife, newly born baby daughter and a mortgage, not without having to move location to bigger shops periodically. Coupled with that, the retail jewellery trade was going through a bad time, but that's another story. So with the chance of a permanent location, better money and the promise of extra work should I need to up my income, I found myself applying for the post of an ordinary rail-man on Hastings Railway Station in East Sussex. My application and interview proved successful, the station manager taking me on, partly based on my families past history in working for the Great Western Railway, GWR, in Swindon, my home town; God's Wonderful Railway as it was known. My father had worked for many years as an electrician's mate, amongst other tasks. This was during the time when steam gave way to diesel. Before that, my grandfather had worked as a boiler maker, one of his brothers too. Even a couple of my brothers worked for the GWR, one starting his draftsman's career in the drawing shop. Many saw my change in work a little demeaning, not really what was expected from someone who had climbed up the career ladder and was heading, so say, for better things. But I'm ever the practical sort and realised that a regular income, along with promotion opportunities, was more important in providing for my family. So, in 1977 I found myself being taught the ropes whilst sweeping platforms, carrying luggage, answering questions and seeing trains in and out of Hastings Railway Station.

Learning on the job is always the best way, as far as I'm concerned. It was a steep learning curve, but quite rewarding when things went well. Being a platform attendant comprised of more than just keeping your space clean, it entailed displaying the details of where a train was stopping at and its destination, (wooden finger boards being used at the time) and knowing the arrival and departure times. At times it was hectic with as many as four trains having to be catered for at the same time with doors to be shut, passengers assisted in and out of the coaches and questions to be answered. Added to this was sweeping out the Ashford train between services. Things sometimes went wrong, trains arriving out of sequence, late starts, doors being left open and the odd simple mistake on my part such as putting the wrong finger board up on display! On the whole though, I enjoyed the work. I got on with the other members of staff and even the passengers. OK, there were some awkward cusses, especially amongst the regular commuters who travelled up to London, but they were few and probably had good cause. No, life on the platform wasn't that bad, but it did entail a shift pattern of three consecutive weeks going from early 6am-4pm, late 3pm-11pm and nights, 10pm–7am, or around those times if memory serves. This proved good for planning ahead on the social front, but proved somewhat disruptive on the domestic front as young children and trying to sleep in the day don't really go together! It was the night shift that proved the worse. After seeing the last trains in at night, getting the drunks safely off and hopefully out of the station, then you were virtually left to your own devices. Oh you had a number of duties to attend to during the night, washing the floors of the public toilets, ticket lobby and concourse, the waiting rooms on the platforms and the various staff rooms. Then there was the brass door handles to polish, the gas fires to attend to and the lights to be turned off and main doors locked. But there was time spare to enjoy the quiet moments, to star gaze, but best of all to watch the resident badgers and foxes along the embankment opposite platform. I would on occasion leave a couple of platform lights on so that I could watch them all the better, but in doing so I ran the risk of upsetting the neighbours, although it didn't stop me! Cold winter nights were best, the animal activity seemed to increase, the snow showing up their footprints and reflecting the light.

Platform work continued for some two years or so before I decided that becoming a train guard offered better prospects, money and variety. However, working on the platform gave me was a deep understanding of just how the railways worked, the routine, rules and regulations and the scams that both the staff and the public got up to. It accustomed me to shift working, stringent time keeping and alternating weather conditions. What I remember in particular is the cold, the wind whistling in off the sea driving rain before it as often as not. It was during such weather that the heavy, wool, surge uniforms came into their own. We were issued with several grey cotton shirts, a couple of red ties, a waistcoat, jacket and two pairs of trousers; to top all that was a long overcoat and peaked hat. When wet the weight was impossible, but the smell of diesel, sweat and ground-in dirt was worse, something that literally stuck with you as nothing could be washed, only dry-cleaned, and that was out of the question. During this time I got to know the supervisors, signalmen and train staff pretty well, and appreciate something of their responsibilities along with the other station staff. Additionally I came into contact with the British Transport Police, from time to time the local police and other emergency services. Then there were the wheel tappers, the solitary figures that walked the sidings checking the coaching stock and trains for wheel defects, their hammers sounding out in the night gave a somehow comforting feel. Platform work taught you who you could rely on in the case of need. That need coming in some strange circumstances, the following example will suffice to illustrate this.

During a week of nights, around Christmas time, I was struggling with bad tooth ache, my dentist not exactly helping by being uncooperative in giving me emergency treatment. The outcome of this was I resorted to seeing my GP for some form of pain killers to get me through the night. Well, my GP gave me more than just pain killers he undertook a session of acupuncture, yes acupuncture! I was reluctant and somewhat doubtful of this approach, my GP admitting that I was to be one of his first patients using this treatment, basically a guinea pig! My main reluctance though was the thought of the needles used in such a procedure, but the pain put that from my mind as I sat down. With my right forearm outstretched and my hand clenched, making a fist, my doctor produced a long needle topped with a slight knob. He then inserted the needle into the muscle between my thumb and forefinger and gentle rotated it backwards and forwards. This produced a slightly uncomfortable sensation, it felt as if something inside my hand was being wound up, then released, most odd. After a few minutes of this the pain had ceased, so had my grimaces! Calm and relaxation returned to me, I felt totally devoid of pain and human again. We looked at each other, my doctor with what might be described as a look of smugness on his face. "Well that seems to have worked. Don't ask me how or why, nobody seems to know, but the results speak for themselves". My doctor's words, or as near as I can remember, was what they say is being honest. I was left a bit at a loss, flabbergasted even. This done, I was given a prescription for some strong pain killers (should I have need of them, as the lasting effects were unknown), and sent on my way.

Later that day the pain returned, the painkillers having to be resorted too. That night I went into work sufficiently dosed up and with more pain killers just in case. By around three in the morning my work was mostly done, the station locked and secure and I was on my own. I took a break for a cuppa in the supervisor's office. Some more pain killers taken, I settled down to read a paper for twenty minutes, but as I did so I slowly became aware of the loss of sensation in my feet, then my legs. This numbness quickly passed through my body and was spreading into my arms. My thoughts of concern started to turn to panic, but my body wouldn't let me move more than my head and hands by now. In desperation I managed to pick up the desktop phone that went through to the signal box at the far end of the station. The signalman was on duty all night like me, so his voice came through like an announcement that I had won the football pools, it gave me not only hope but the reassurance that help was at hand. A little later people appeared, but by now I was in a semi-conscious state and barely able to relate my plight, but the tablets on the desk next to my tea told them what they needed to know. A phone call to my doctor at that hour was not too well received, but he was able to reassure all concerned that my condition would improve with a full recovery later that day. A taxi was got and I was taken home to recover, my wife being somewhat surprised and alarmed by my arrival in the early hours. This episode was, and has been, the only time I've ever over dosed, the direct result of pain causing desperation and confusion. I may not owe my life to that signalman, but I was pretty glad he was around and managed the situation calmly and efficiently.

One aspect of railway work that was to prove galling to me was the requirement that you had to belong to a trade union. This was a legal requirement at the time, the monthly subs (subscriptions), being taken directly out of your pay via the wages department. The result of this was that when first entering the service, the representatives of the various unions came to you in order to obtain your membership. The competition was fierce as I remember. Well I settled for the National Union of Railwaymen (NUR) as being the least proactive, hopefully meaning fewer days off on strike! You must remember we had just gone through several years in the 1970's of industrial action, culminating in the miners' strike and the three day week. This had had a huge impact during my former career, with reduced opening hours, security problems and loss of earnings. I was not happy about this enforcement on me of what I perceived to be an infringement upon on my personal freedom. But, and this is the point, I had no option if I wanted to work on BR. So I became a member of the NUR, but only attended a couple of union meetings, more in order to understand just how it functioned at grass roots level. These meetings were held in a room above the pub on the concourse up to Hastings Railway Station. In my naivety, I had not questioned the finer points, the nitty gritty of being a union member. I was totally unaware that a political levy formed part of my subscriptions, and that they were used to fund the Labour party, a party I did not and never have supported! This realisation came over a year into my employment and the knowledge that I was at liberty to withhold such payments. When I brought this up with the union representative and said I not only wanted my political levy to stop, but I also wanted the former payments refunded as I had not had this drawn to my attention when he first press-ganged me into membership, he was none too happy and very uncooperative. Well the situation dragged on for some weeks, the levy being stopped, but the refund being questioned. After some more words with the union rep. followed up with discussions with BR, the refund was sanctioned. The outcome of this was that a cheque was made out in my favour, to be collected and signed for at the next branch meeting of the union. I was not at all happy with this and told the union rep. so, on account of his chasing me in my place of employment originally, so I therefore wanted this matter dealt with at work, not involving me in wasting my own time attending a meeting out of work hours. He refused! So more words passed between me, BR and the union, the outcome, the union rep. was forced to comply with my wishes. This was not the last time I had to stand up against the union on my own behalf, BR management too, for that matter.

My thoughts had however turned to more demanding work with more responsibility, which left me with a couple of options if I wanted to continue working for BR. One was to go for management training within BR but this didn't really appeal as it meant many years learning the ropes and having to move around, basically the same reasons why I had given up on the retail jewellery trade. My second option was getting onto a Guard's course, which lasted six weeks, and if successful would mean being stationed in a local depot. The good thing about being a guard was that it had the added interest of travelling round during the course of your duty and at the same time dealing with the general public. Both these aspects of the job appealed to me, along with not being constantly at the beck and call of your immediate 'superior'. So I made further enquiries and requested that I be considered for a placement on the next course. Whether for my credentials, or to get me out of their hair, I was accepted for training and duly prepared to commute each day up to Beckenham in Kent. With my training and exam results proving successful, I became a guard. This was to lead to five years serving the commuters and general public of Hastings, a period during which many changes occurred and incidents happened.

This brings me back to where we came in, racing towards the level crossing gates closed against us at Warehorn, with nowhere to hide! A second quick look out of the offside window confirmed my previous observations, cars were crossing in front of us, the gates were closed against us and there was no way we could possibly stop short of the gates due to our speed, the fall of the track towards the crossing and our inertia. I called up the driver on the intercom, but as was usual when moving at speed communication was virtually impossible, we however managed to confirm that all brakes should be applied. The emergency chain pull brake applied, I then proceeded to apply the hand-brake located in the centre of the guard's brake; this is no easy matter when the train is moving, the screw seeming to go on for ever, very reminiscent of the opening sequence in BBC's Have I Got News for You with the Russian closing off the oil pipe line to Europe. That finally done I once more looked out of the window, this time to see the gatekeeper working frantically to open the gates whilst yet another car crossed the lines! There was nothing more I could do, and no time to warn the passengers (no passenger announcement system), besides, the configuration of the coaching stock wouldn't let me get through the entire train. With the driver continuing to sound the horn, I sank to the ground with my back braced against the wall of the brake facing the rear of the train and waited.

The horn suddenly fell silent, the wheels had locked and slid along the rails before slowly coming to a halt. Once on my feet, and subconsciously realising that we were still upright, I looked out of the window. The crossing was several yards behind us, the gatekeeper standing dazed alongside the rails. My first priority was to see that the passengers were all OK, then to secure the train by making it safe against any possibility of another running into us. With this in mind I went through the first coach, thankfully no one was hurt, just shocked. Dropping down to the line I quickly confirmed the same in the forward coach and then met up with the driver. We walked back to the crossing and there was what was left of one of the gates, basically matchwood. The other lay in parts, a large chunk of which was balanced precariously on the gatekeeper's car that was parked next to his hut. The hut door was open, within was the gatekeeper's TV blasting out some programme, no doubt part of the reason why he had not closed the gates against traffic! Quite why he hadn't registered the bell that gave warning of our departure from Ham Street station some five minutes earlier I don't know, but he hadn't. Turning to the shocked gatekeeper, then back to the remains of the gates and to his battered car, no words could sum up just how near we had come to disaster. Luckily for us we had not been derailed, no car or pedestrian had been hit, other than the gatekeeper's, and the passengers along with the driver were OK. He, like me, had ducked down at the last moment in fear of the windscreen coming in on him. With the situation somewhat clearer, I went off back along the line some five hundred yards and began placing detonators one hundred yards apart. This was normal procedure in such cases, a way of warning any following train of your presence. But I had only laid two when recalled, the driver having spoken with the signalman at Ham Street who was now fully aware of what had happened and could confirm the line behind was secure. This was the first, and only, time I ever had need to use detonators, twelve of which we carried in a canister in our bag everywhere when on duty. These detonators are caps some 2inches in diameter and about half an inch thick, full of gunpowder. They have two leaded strips attached that allow you to clamp them to the rail so that any train passing over will detonate them, thereby warning of an obstruction ahead. With little more to be done, and knowing both lines were clear of debris, we continued to Rye, then onto Hastings where I filed a report and waited on any repercussions.

The above incident was just one of many that led to the installation of unmanned automatic half barriers (AHB's) at isolated road crossings. Those at Warehorne, along with others on this line, were late in coming, due mainly to the reluctance on the part of BR to invest whilst there were doubts as to the line being kept open. Incidentally, I have not been able to locate an official report concerning this incident. It appears as if none were ever made for whatever reason, most strange!

Guards training.

Attendance on the Guards course was to last six weeks, the first three of which were shared with the Shunters course. This comprised of the making up of both passenger and goods trains and the health and safety rules that were essential in maintaining a safe working environment for both staff and the travelling public alike. An exam was to be taken at the end of these three weeks, another on completion of the Guards unit.

The courses were centred on Beckenham in Kent, which required a lot of travelling each day back and forth from Hastings. Some days were spent in other locations undergoing firefighting training and the coupling and uncoupling of trains for example. It was this aspect of the Shunters' course that sorted out the participants. Getting down on the track and standing between two engines can be a daunting experience for some. The buffers loom large at face level whilst the couplings are massive and can weigh a ton. Different types of couplings demanded different approaches to working, the simple chain links on goods wagons requiring a cross between brute strength and a rhythmical action when using their own weight to provide the inertia needed to swing them up and into place. This proved impossible for some, not only the odd women on the course, but quite a few of the men too. The secret was to use the coupling's own weight as I've said, otherwise I doubt if I could have managed it as I stand only 5ft 5inches tall and at the time weighed under eight stone. The pivoted couplings on the diesel units were even heavier, but here again, a swing action involving technique, not brawn, was all that was needed. The other aspect that got some participants rattled was the air brakes. When breaking the vacuum air pipe over your knee, or between your hands, in order to separate units, a tremendous noise along with a mini explosion took place. This took some getting used to, that and the dirt and grease that accompanied the job. But what unnerved some, was being in close proximity to the units when they were drawn apart, worse still when they were being brought together! It was at this point that some dropped out of the course, natural wastage you might say.

Firefighting training was mainly classroom orientated, getting to know the different sorts of extinguishers carried on the units, and their different uses; one for general purpose use, another for electrical fires etc. Practical sessions were carried out over one day up in Norwood, if I remember correctly. This crash course enabled limited experience of using and operating various extinguishers on different types of fire. You weren't really expected to tackle fires apart from the odd waste bin going up, or perhaps in response to some other minor incident, but there is no alternative to the real thing, so being confronted by smoke, heat and live flames was all to the good. Having spent time as a voluntary fireman in more recent years, I now realise just how basic this training was and not really fit for purpose. It only played lip service to the issue and has probably been greatly improved upon since then. Amongst other things, ticket inspection, revenue collection and public announcements were dealt with, again in a blanket cover sort of way. The various trains we were likely to encounter were looked at, whilst signalling and communications along with braking systems studied in greater depth. There was a lot to learn, more to commit to memory and home-work by the armful! I made it a rule to study my home-work whilst travelling to and from home on the train each day. What didn't sink in then, never would, as a wife and young family meant that home-life made it nigh-on impossible to study at home.

The Shunters course went off well, but I found the detail to working out the combined tare weight of loaded goods trains rather tiresome, let alone complicated, maths not being a strong point of mine. As is the case with many such courses, you cover far more ground than you're likely to ever need, especially as I was looking at working out of St. Leonards West Marina depot where I would only be working passenger trains. Still I persevered and came through the exam with flying colours as they say. Mind you, the pass level required was only around 55% and plenty of time was allowed. I did so well because I sat out the full three hours of the exam, taking the time to go over my answers and refine, or correct, them; whereas many of the other students got up and left when they felt they had finished, so as to get down the pub for an early lunch! The Guards course followed a similar pattern, the exam proving to be fairly straight forward with equally good results for me. What I think BR really wanted to see from these results, was not a total knowledge of all aspects of train working, but those areas that mattered on a day to day basis, the rest could be checked up on in the many bulletins, notices and changes to timetables that were issued daily, weekly and monthly in-house. Working schedules and timetables played a very important part of the Guards course, so knowing how to read them and where to look for information was paramount. Part of the course dealt with revenue protection in some detail, as guards were expected to check the ticket validity of those travelling on trains, to be able to issue tickets and take money. But, and this was the primary point of importance, Guards were just that, guards, to protect the welfare of the public and those using the trains, the trains themselves coming second. Obviously good working practice reduced risks and avoided dangers. This basic understanding of the main aims of a guard, and the accepted responsibilities that went with the job, remained with me throughout my time spent working for BR, that being from late in the 1970's through to 1984.

Having passed the exams was not the end of training. Before you could pass out as a guard you were required to carry out route training, both on the job with another time-served guard and on your own over a period of some weeks, focusing on the area you were likely to have to work. This proved a good time for me as I was left to my own devices and the freedom to travel the region getting to know not only the stations, sidings, level-crossings, speed restrictions and signalling, but to have the odd 'jolly'. By 'jolly' I mean the odd away-day under the pretext of route knowledge. One such 'jolly' took me out of my region, via Ashford, and on down to Dover. Arriving in Dover I took advantage of the staff-room facilities, stowing my large leather guard's bag, before setting off into the town to explore. Incidentally, it was this bag that acted as a sort of open ticket when travelling on the trains, provided you were in uniform. No questions were asked, which gave you free reign to wander anywhere you wished. This early freedom didn't last long. When it was felt you were sufficiently knowledgeable, and even if you weren't time was precious, you had to begin to earn your keep. So, the honeymoon period over, I was officially assigned to my new depot, St. Leonards West Marina, a few miles west of Hastings in East Sussex, where I lived.

A baptism of fire.

Well, the day dawned when I was to take up my new post as a fully-fledged Guard. I had been kitted out with differing uniform from that of an ordinary railwayman, the hat had white trim, the shirts were blue and a full set of waterproofs were provided including a great coat type overcoat, mac and a high visibility vest. Interestingly, you were expected to provide your own footwear. There were lots of additional bits and pieces, other than the whistle and carriage key which also gave access to guards' brakes, and was general issue.

These additional bits consisted of a pair of flags, one red, one green, mounted on wooden handles, a heavy square shaped hand-lamp, with adjustable colour lenses, and a white-metal canister containing twelve explosive detonators. This last item was not only bulky, but weighty too. Added to all this was a set of timetables, advance notices of working and diversions and a rule book. These items were meant to be carried at all times when working trains, so a large sturdy leather, satchel type, bag was provided to hold them all, which incidentally allowed the lamp to be attached too as well. When filled with the above, it left precious little room for your flask and sandwiches! This last factor, along with the weight, led to many guards, including myself, leaving many of the timetables, and any other unnecessary items, back in their locker in the guard's room at the depot. This was a slightly risky business as you never quite knew when you might get diverted, taken off your duty and put on another, or simply needed your waterproofs. On top of all this you were issued with a small float, the money required to provide change when issuing tickets, a fares chart and a pair of ticket nippers used for cancelling tickets, or showing that you had checked them. These nippers resembled a pair of metal pliers and along with a docket book, the pad for issuing hand-written tickets, proved to be essential kit when working late night trains or rural routes where there were unmanned stations. These smaller working items you had to carry about your person, so the multitude of pockets in your uniform came into their own. What I found rather strange was not being issued with a watch! Some of the older guards carried pocket watches that had been issued to them in the past. These were hand-wound pieces, mostly very accurate and robust. This peeved me somewhat, as I had my grandfather's silver double 'Albert' watch chain and fob which I wore on my waistcoat, my whistle attached to one end.

If I remember rightly, my first few days were spent acquainting myself with procedures, telephone numbers and names; there were so many people's names and positions to learn, whom to call if this or that happened, or you needed further information and where you were expected to be at any given time. My base was officially the tiny guards' room located at the northern end of the carriage sheds in St. Leonards West Marina depot. Here we were expected to start our duties and check the daily changing notices, store our gear in the lockers provided and be in attendance if undertaking a 'spare' duty. This last item was just that, you were spare in case another guard failed to turn in for their duty, or available to cover any unforeseen eventualities. This was never a good duty as it meant sitting in this cramped, smelly, claustrophobic room for up to eight hours! When faced with 'spare' duty you made sure you had a good book or something to while away the time. Unlike the driver's mess at the other end of the depot, we didn't have room for cosy arm chairs, let alone a TV or cooking area. No this was a purely utilitarian space, the window looking out onto the embankment where the engines were refuelled, the access door straight out into the carriage sheds where the engines were warmed up and cleaning was undertaken; so, all in all a very noisy, dark, smelly place at the start and finish of the day. You did everything you could to get put on a job, or relocated to Hastings to cover when the initial start-up times had passed and everything seemed to be running smoothly.

We had twenty odd different duties running consecutively, which meant twenty odd different start and finish times, after which it would start all over again! This wasn't quite so bad as it sounds as it meant you knew which duty you were on well in advance, to the point of being able to plan days off and holidays. Swopping duties was quite OK too, provided you got it approved in advance with your supervisor, so that allowed for flexibility. I don't know if it was purely down to when I joined the guards' roster that I found myself having Christmas's off, but having to work the last train down from London on New Year's Eve, which meant not getting home to nearer two in the morning; still, more of the implications of that later. The shift pattern fell into roughly two sessions, earlies, starting any time between four-thirty and eight and finishing around twelve-thirty and five pm. and lates, starting from say two to six in the afternoon with finishes accordingly eight to nine hours later. These were of course the official times, but some duties allowed for later starts or earlier finishes! Such 'perks' usually relied upon other guards covering for you, some from other depots. Off course such action was basically fraud, as you were obtaining payment for hours not worked. This was new to me, and something I wasn't altogether comfortable with. But it was the accepted norm, often expected and something you did for others in the knowledge that your turn would come round. No doubt this type of 'perk' still goes on, even allowing for tightening up and efficiency drives. When it comes to being clever, the ordinary working chap is perhaps the smartest, provided his conscience allows it!

If working a train from the depot, then extra time was allowed at the start of the duty to prepare it and make sure all was ready for service. This time was also meant to allow for checking the notice boards for any last minute changes to schedules and working. Basically the guard was required to walk the length of the train, both inside and out, checking for any obvious defects, uncleaned areas and missed restocking of toilets etc. This was carried out whilst the engines were being warmed up by the driver and he was carrying out his checks. When satisfied all was OK, then a series of brake checks were gone through with the driver. These checks were undertaken with the guard at one end and the driver at the other of the train, the internal intercom being used to communicate both by talking and a series of recognised bell pushes. On the Diesel Electrical Mechanical Units (DEMU), an engine was located at both ends of the carriages. These in turn could be coupled together to form longer trains, hence the need to check that the vacuum brake systems had built up to the correct pressures before moving out of the carriage sheds. It was whilst still a novice, having only just passed out, that I was to fall foul of a driver who was running late. I had carried out my checks, but he decided to move out of the carriage shed before the brakes were up to pressure. Whilst still within the sidings this was not a real problem as speeds were low and time spent moving into position prior to going out onto the permanent way, the actual public service rails, would result in the correct levels being met. Unsure of myself, I let this go but watched the dials as we headed towards the far end of the siding, prepared to hit the brakes if needs be. Coming to a halt, I waited for the signal that would let us move off and out onto the permanent way. However, the driver wanting to make up for lost time, opened up the regulator (basically the throttle) and moved off at speed before the signal had turned to green. It was at this point that I decided to act and called the driver to stop. He reacted correctly and eased off the regulator and applied the brakes, but then once again began to accelerate before the signal had changed. Yet again I called him to stop but this time he continued, the signal turning to green only as we drew close to it, by which time we were beyond the point of no return and committed. We were running empty coaching stock through to Hastings to provide a passenger service, which meant that we would have to change ends.

This should have been the opportunity to sort things out but somehow that didn't happen, which left us both angry. The outcome was not satisfactory, the driver feeling that I had over-reacted, and I for my part being un-nerved by the experience. I had allowed the situation to get out of hand and also made an enemy of the driver. This was not to be the last incident in which my lack of experience was to land me in an awkward situation.

Virtually all our duties entailed working diesels, DEMU's, this was mainly down to the Hastings to Tunbridge Wells and Hastings to Ashford lines not being electrified. The only electric train we were rostered to work was one from Hastings to Eastbourne. This rare occurrence had missed my attention, so when I leapt aboard what I thought was the train I had to work up from Tonbridge to London, for the first time, I was somewhat perplexed when the guard carried on working. We chatted away for some minutes before the penny dropped. I had in fact boarded an earlier train that was running late. My stupidity knew no bounds as this was an electric train to boot! Ordinarily such a mistake would have no consequences, but of course I was now en-route to Sevenoaks and there would be no guard to work my train. It was not possible to let the supervisor at Tonbridge know what had happened until I got to Sevenoaks, no mobiles those days, so cover would not be forthcoming straightaway which meant my train being delayed. Well as it happens the guard, who I was supposed to relieve, was able to work the train up to Sevenoaks where I resumed my duty. The outcome of this was a loss of face and much embarrassment on my part, but at least not too much harm was done as all trains at the time were running late out of Tonbridge anyway.

These then are just two of the many incidents that went to help turn me into an experienced guard, one that knew how to cope as and when events out of the blue materialised, or new ways of working were encountered. More pressing in many ways, however, was the actual day to day business of getting into work. With some duties commencing in the middle of the night, well before any public transport was running, you had to make your own arrangements. At first I relied on my bicycle to cover the four miles or so into work, the first mile being all downhill, then a flat ride along the seafront. But with a stiff bracing head wind and driving rain, it was no joke on occasions, besides the last mile home was all uphill! I soon acquired a moped to reduce the effort and the time. This proved adequate, but really bad conditions still meant you were like as not to get to work wet through, not the best way to start a duty. As time passed, my wages increased due to overtime working, a car was finally got following driving lessons and a second test proving successful. What a difference a car made, not only to getting into work, but life in general. No more reliance on public transport, the weekly shop with three young children manageable and greater flexibility. Of course with greater affluence and private transport comes a decline in public transport, exactly what paid my wages! Another aspect of owning a car was that the free travel on the railways that formed part of the overall wage structure now seemed less desirable, thereby reducing its worth. But even once I owned a car my early starts still could prove difficult, with the rare occurrence of ice and snow making getting to work nigh on impossible. I remember having to walk on more than one occasion, the road conditions proving too treacherous for mechanised transport.

Everyday working.

What follows is a flavour of the ordinary, everyday, nitty-gritty of working trains during the first half of the 1980's. Being a guard was not any more at the top of my wish list as say being a train driver, the latter being most boys dream job at the time. But in fact, being a guard was far more preferable to that of being a driver for me personally. As a guard you got to work with the public, walk around, get on and off trains and generally be active. The poor old driver, however, basically had to sit where he was, being at the mercy of the signals and my stop and stop commands, getting little exercise, just fat!

A normal duty would begin with checking the last minute notices upon arrival in the Guards Room, the previously printed changes having been looked at the day before. Based on any changes, the necessary timetables, notices and other equipment would be packed into your guard's bag along with sandwiches etc. Then it was off out into the carriage sheds to check out your train. This was a necessary part of the routine, one that if you cut corners had a nasty way of biting back! Happy or otherwise, once having walked the length of the train you then had to walk back through it ideally, checking this time for any obvious things out of place or missing, for example the firefighting equipment carried. Sometimes the cleaners had done a rush job, for whatever reason, so that had to be corrected, usually upon arrival in Hastings or wherever was the starting point of the service. Then it was up front into the drivers cab, usually walking through the engine room via the guard's brake. Later, the access from the guard's brake was sealed off on all units in an attempt to reduce sound, thereby reducing the associated health and safety issues. Having called up the driver on the intercom, who was by now in his cab at the other end of the train, we proceeded to carry out the required brake tests. Part of the test called for you to evacuate the air brake and then watch as it came back up to the required pressure. This was perhaps the most important part of the safety checks, yet one some staff seemed to think it OK to shortcut. If all was well, then it was time to shunt onto the sidings in readiness for going through to Hastings. This was one of the few times that as guard you sat up front in the train, the driver effectively driving from the rear and bringing the train to a halt short of the buffers, well that was the plan! As you then set off, you moved through to the guard's brake and started to prepare your log book having made notes of the unit numbers, the driver's name and any other points that might be required later. Of course, following the blanking off of the engine room doors, this had to wait until arrival in Hastings.

Most of the trains we worked out of St. Leonards West Marina depot were commuter trains, serving the mainline routes up to London Charing Cross and Cannon Street via Tonbridge. On the early duties we carried the ever growing numbers of commuters up to town, on the lates, back again. Some services stopped at Tonbridge, returning to Hastings, others were coupled up to other services, or split and worked separately. The organisation, train movements and logistics required to keep the services running smoothly, have the train crews in the right place and keep everything to time was an art form in itself. Much of this was down to the people on the ground, the signalmen and supervisors in particular. But as with anything so intricate, every person on the staff had a part to play in the service and formed an important cog in the wheels. You were very reliant on the expertise and cooperation of those about you, the goodwill of the travelling public and your own knowledge.

Prior to setting off at the start of a public service, as the guard, likewise the driver, you were expected to check that the correct destination was displayed in the lit up panel on the front of the train. This might not seem an important task, but it helped not only the public to identify what service they were boarding but also staff, including signalmen and supervisors to keep a check on traffic movements. When ready to leave the station after first checking all the doors were secure, including the offside ones if possible, the time of departure was right and that the signal was off, in other words it was safe to move off, you usually made a quick check with the platform staff if the station was manned. It may sound a bit belt and braces, but believe me, you needed to have your wits about you in order to avoid accidents such as open doors hitting anyone or the driver, momentarily forgetting himself and, moving off on your signal without first checking the starter or advance starter signal was off. The latter was an ever present risk, but drivers had such operating systems drummed into them that this virtually never happened. It was actually the driver's responsibility to work according to the signal in this case, the guard only notifying the driver by his signal, usually a bell ring, he was ready to leave. On DEMU's a box was located over the guard brake doors that had a pull lever bell connected direct to the driver's cab, that's why you often saw the guard hanging out of the brake's door or window. This bell could only be operated if it had been switched on, the key for which was issued to guards and had to be inserted into a switch box located over the sloping table within the guard's brake. Normal procedure was to have this key attached by a long chain, or line, to your guard's bag. The bag was then hung by the coat hook next to the switch, or on the floor. It was always a good idea to carry a spare key in case you were separated from your bag. I remember one particular occasion when my wife along with our two youngest children was travelling on my train. Our daughter would have been around two years old and was fascinated by the starter bell. When all was ready I picked her up and helped her to pull the starter lever, the train lurched forward much to my daughter's pleasure!

Additional to the electric starter bell was the hand held flag (green for go, red for stop) the whistle, along with a raised hand, or the hand held lamp at night or in fog. All methods allowed for greater flexibility in working a train. Various bell codes and the number of whistle blasts or lamp flashes commuted your instruction to the driver. When carrying out ticket checks, going through the train a carriage at a time, the short space of time between stations on some lines required the guard to alight onto the platform at odd points during stops. Once clear to depart again, then a hand-signal, or one of the other signals, meant you could re-join the train anywhere and not be confined to operating just from the guard's brake; this was crucial when working a six car, particularly a twelve car train. Such working was also necessary to maintain timing, especially on unstaffed stations or halts, but more of this later. Of course a good working partnership was required between the guard and the driver as once a signal under these conditions was given, then it was very difficult to abort and get the driver to stop again should a door suddenly fly open, or your sight line was obscured. A good driver would keep his head out of his cab on the look-out for any problems in all weather conditions. Some would even stop the train and attend to an open door if it had gone unnoticed, or was just behind the cab, thereby saving time. Another aspect of this way of working was if the driver opened the regulator fully, then you were at risk of being left behind. There was the odd occasion when this very nearly happened to me, one in particular requiring me to run and step-up into a fast accelerating train, clinging to the open door. But that wasn't the end of my dilemma, the gathering speed of the train made it almost beyond me to close the door. No, a good working relationship with your driver was essential otherwise he could make life hell for you!

Once on the move the guard was expected to keep a look out for any dangers, for example an open door on a passing train, a signal being passed at red, pedestrians on the line at unmanned rural footpath and farm crossings. All these things held their dangers not only to those on your train, but others too. You got to know where such dangers were likely to be encountered, but most of the time routine ticket inspection and answering passengers questions were the main things that filled your time, that and keeping your daily log along with your time sheets up to date. The log book was really quite important, it let you make notes of any odd occurrences, keep track of changes in working, record incidents and generally put your thoughts and observations down on paper. You never really knew as and when you might need to refer back to it, likewise it could be asked to be seen by management at any time. Make no mistake your log was your memory, at times crucial when answering later queries, or worse still, public complaints. Time sheets were a constant bit of the job, keeping them up to date so that you were paid not only for the trains worked, but for preparation time, holiday working, unsociable hours and most importantly, overtime. Your basic wage covered the 40 hour standard week, which in 1980 averaged £3,000 per annum but the add-ons made all the difference to your take home pay. Of course these timesheets were also a statement of what trains you had physically worked, so should there ever be a query, you could be brought to book and dealt with accordingly.

When time permitted, between stations, it was expected that you went through the train checking passengers' tickets. This part of the job was to cause some consternation at times as it left you isolated from the driver, with no communication, but also reduced your primary function which was to guard the train and its passengers. Ticket inspection, however, served several purposes the first was an endeavour to reduce payment avoidance, secondly it gave an opportunity to answer any queries a passenger might have and thirdly, it enabled the guard to advise passengers about train changes and alighting points if need be. But perhaps the most important aspect was being seen by the public and making yourself available to them. This was important as for many, old and infirm passengers in particular, it gave reassurance. For some passengers though, your presence was like a 'red rag to a bull' as they say. In packed commuter trains you had to physically push through and being asked to show a ticket or pass was not altogether easy to do. So you were considered by some as a 'bloody nuisance', 'a jumped up pip-squeak' or the like; but most realised that it was an ordeal for the guard too, that you were only doing your job and that by doing so it helped reduce fares. Well that was the theory, but truth be told, it really had little impact on revenue protection. Some guards had passed out as a Guard/Conductor. One in particular in our depot wore his cap badge proudly and acted as surrogate uncle to many of the young novices like myself. He could work a train like no other, seldom causing umbrage and often defusing potential conflict. For a role model you need look no further. What really made a difference to revenue protection was the TTI's, the Travelling Ticket Inspectors' that would suddenly appear out of the blue and do a thorough check throughout the train. It was them that maintained a sense of nervousness in the so called 'fare dodger', especially when a couple worked together or enlisted the guards help. Not all guards liked TTI's as some felt intimidated by them, the same also thought that it reflected upon their ability to do their job and in some cases they'd be right! For my part I welcomed them, but then I tended to strike a middle path, neither being too pushy or allowing people to ride roughshod over me when it came to ticket checks.

A final word on ticket checks won't go amiss. We were issued with a simple docket book, basically a receipt pad with carbon copies. When issuing a ticket we therefore retained the carbon copy in the pad, giving the punter the top copy, after first using the ticket nips to authenticate it. Cash was the order of the day, checks being accepted upon production of a banker's card and further identification. Change was given, hence a need for a float. When a ticket was required simply for the local service, a scale of charges could be referred to which you kept about your person, but should a ticket be wanted for travel outside your region, then problems arose. One way of overcoming such difficulties was to issue a ticket only to the furthest mainline station, leaving the passenger to purchase a further ticket. This often would result in the passenger having to pay more, a further inducement to having purchased a ticket before setting out in the first place! Such ticketing was unfair when the passenger had come from an unstaffed station, or where the ticket office was closed. It was on such occasions I would make the extra effort and work out the best price, which inevitably meant having to go back to the guards brake to consult the fare books. My best ticket issued was for a return to some far flung place in Scotland if I remember correctly.

During a normal working day, you might have to work a train up to London and back down to the south coast which would account for the best part of the shift. Some duties involved a break in, say, Royal Tunbridge Wells or Tonbridge others might involve working trains through to Ashford or Eastbourne along with other local services. The work was varied and presented interest and not the odd incident, to which I'll give some examples later. The commuter services up to Cannon Street would often require that the train was then worked empty back over the Thames and round to Charing Cross via Waterloo. This particular duty you needed to be alert as it was quite common to be stopped in Waterloo East station where the odd commuter was not adverse to attempting to board the empty train, although the lights were turned off and the display panel would say 'Not in Service'. Cannon Street also presented a long break on one of the duties, time to go off exploring. I've often strolled off up Cannon Street to view St. Pauls or the Roman temple to Mithras. My best sorties though, were to go down onto the Thames foreshore if the tide was out, mud-larking! This was not a good idea really as you got muddy shoes, occasionally your overcoat too as a result of crouching down to study something, but the finds made it all worthwhile. Being the site of what is believed was the former Governor's palace of Roman Britain the Thames alongside Cannon Street offered the chance of making an exciting find. However, Roman finds eluded me, but I did build up quite a good collection of old clay smoking pipes, or rather their bowls, over several such visits. This was a highlight for me, one of the perks that made the job so worthwhile.

Food and rest breaks were built into your duties, the one at Charing Cross being a favourite of mine. As with Cannon Street, I would go off exploring, but here there was the added benefit of a good large staff canteen. It wasn't so much the cheap fry-ups and butties that tempted me, but the location. Set high up over the concourse and ticket lobby, with windows all round, I just loved to people watch. The London terminus stations were always busy with tourists and people going about their everyday lives, cosmopolitan and full of energy, I loved it. Both Royal Tunbridge Wells and Tonbridge stations also offered good locations for exploring during breaks. The former gave quick access to the common for fresh air and exercise, the Pantiles for shopping; the latter had its fair share of interesting old buildings with the castle grounds providing more open space. Most of the time meal breaks were spent in rather drab staff rooms, so if time and the weather permitted I would get out and about, even if that meant just ten or twenty minutes. It was during such sorties that I came to know the finer points of the locations, by that I mean the local vernacular architecture, an interest that has always formed an important part of my life.

With the end of a late duty often came the working of an empty train back to the depot at St. Leonards West Marina. In preparation, if the train was to be refuelled and washed, the guard would walk through the train prior to reaching Hastings and close all the windows, check for any drunks who had fallen asleep and generally making the unit secure for going through the automatic washers located on the former site of West Marina station. These checks were repeated in Hastings station both by the guard and the platform staff, the closing of the windows being paid particular attention along with checking that no passengers remained on the train. I well remember walking back through an empty unit as we passed through the washers, usually at slow speed, but some drivers went at quite a pace in an endeavour to get their duty over that bit quicker. On the odd occasion someone did manage to stay aboard, either by concealing themselves in a toilet, if the checks had not been thorough, but like as not, due to not being able to wake them in Hastings. On one such occasion I remember arranging for a reception committee to meet the unit in the depot so as to manhandle a very sound asleep drunk off the premises. In some cases, to maintain timings and not to hold up other services, such action was necessary. Where possible we heaved drunks off in Hastings so that they could either be left to sleep it off, or have the opportunity of getting a taxi home. The big problem was those that had overslept, missing their station with no way of being put on the next return service, that is, not until the next day! Having once been the person responsible for securing Hastings station overnight, I knew what a problem such punters proved. They were officially not allowed to stay on the premises, but I must admit to letting the odd one bed down in the waiting room on a cold night provided they behaved themselves. This particular problem was made worse around Christmastime when office parties were in full swing. Then there were the small group of commuters who propped up the bar in the buffet car on a regular basis. We got to know who they were and, where possible, woke them up before their station, but you couldn't be minding them all the time.

Lost property was a common factor that formed part of your duties. Either you were handed things by members of the public, or you came across the odd item whilst working a train. The usual finds were umbrellas, hats, scarves and the odd coat. Two examples will suffice to illustrate this, the first a strange find made at Orpington. I had just checked for any open doors and was returning to my brake van when I noticed a bread knife lying on the platform! Not the normal sort of thing you expect to come across. Being late evening and quiet, I picked the knife up and put it into one of the large inside pockets of my overcoat. Once on our way I was able to examine the knife. It was a common sort of bread knife, a long serrated steel blade with a swept-down tip and ornate carved wooden handle, the sort most people owned of a certain age, and still do! Several thoughts went through my head, primarily, that it might be a weapon from a mugging that had been cast aside. But, after some more thought I discounted this idea, after all, the blade had no real point and was not really ideal for concealing about one's person! So it remained a mystery and I accordingly put it back in my overcoat pocket. It was a few days later that I rediscovered the knife, I had completely forgotten all about it. Having heard no reports of any incidents, or wishing to look a bit stupid, I never reported it and took the knife home where it landed up in my tool box.

The next lost property example was quite common, but in this case a bit out of the ordinary. I had just finished working a commuter service into Cannon Street station and was going through the train on the lookout for a discarded newspaper when I came across a fat leather wallet. Opening it I was confronted by loads of paper money along with credit cards. What was I to do? I was loath to hand it over to the platform staff as I was unsure of whether it would be handed into lost property intact. I know that sounds bad, but such things did happen. So, with time running out before I was to resume my duty, I found a member of the platform staff and asked him to witness what I was going to do. As we stood there I counted the cash. It came to somewhere just short of four hundred pounds! That represented over two weeks take home pay to me at the time, so quite a sum. Also within the wallet was at least three credit cards, but no address of the owner, but from that on the cards it was possible to deduce he was a foreigner on holiday. Having done that, I got the member of staff to sign my log book and gave him a duplicate of the details. That wallet went with me back to Hastings where I went through all the same procedures, but this time with the lost property office. Well weeks went by and I heard no news of the wallet being claimed. More time went by and the wallet remained unclaimed. Finally I received a formal notification by BR that the wallet and its contents had been kept by BR. No reward was offered me as I was staff and could not be seen to be benefiting from my position. Well that really rankled with me, after all, I could have said nothing and kept the wallet. At the very least I could have handed in the wallet, minus the cash, and no one could have accused me of theft. No, BR was not my favourite employer at that moment, even a 10% reward would have been nice, a substantial amount towards my monthly mortgage. You have to ask yourself on occasions like that whether honesty really is the best policy, but then I still do believe that.

On many of the duties you finished working a train and travelling back to the depot either on the empty units, or via West St. Leonards Station and having to walk from there. Just occasionally you could head straight home, but often as not, you had to return to the depot if only to pick up the car. The walk back from West St. Leonards Station was around a mile, but on a cold wet night, at the end of a duty, it was the last thing you wanted.

Mortality & injuries.

Dealing with such a subject is necessary when looking at the everyday life of a railway guard as it forms part of the experience. With the above in mind, I thought it better to address this area now, rather than leave it to last and end on a low.

Accidents were thankfully few and far between, but they did happen. Some resulted in death, others in emergencies that had to be dealt with as and when. Then there were the incidents where passengers or staff fell ill and medical help was required. I highlighted such an incident earlier that happened to me whilst working nights on Hastings Station. Whilst we received some basic first aid training, it was far from adequate. Now I would suppose such training is given more prominence. Of course passengers fell ill, often heart attacks, fits or asthma attacks were encountered. Thankfully I never experienced the first, well not in my capacity as a guard, but I do remember a particular incident whilst working a commuter train up to London. We had left Orpington en-route for Cannon Street, with no scheduled stops between. Shortly after there was a knock on the brake-van door, a passenger stood there ashen faced. She requested that I went with her to attend another passenger who had collapsed. When we got back to the casualty, a small crowd had gathered. My limited first-aid knowledge, coupled with common sense, told me to clear the area. That done it soon became apparent that the man in front of me was having some kind of fit. A little more questioning of those around confirmed my suspicions that this was an epileptic fit, or seizure. Another person, with more medical experience than me, took control of the situation and turned the casualty on their side whilst restraining them and preventing them from swallowing their tongue. The dilemma now was what was to be done? Although in all probability the seizures would pass and the casualty recover slowly, that was not certain. With no stops scheduled, and no way of ringing ahead short of contacting the driver to stop at the next signal and use the phone to speak with the signalman, I had to make a decision.

Leaving the casualty in the care of his fellow passengers I returned to the brake-van and called up the driver. We agreed that he would make an unscheduled stop at London Bridge Station, being the nearest location where medical assistance could easily attend. I knew this course of action would create problems, particularly with the commuters expecting to arrive in Cannon Street at their normal time. Well we duly came to a halt in London Bridge Station, not altogether unusual when schedules were a little out. I immediately requested an ambulance from the station supervisor and we awaited its arrival. During the wait several commuters left the train, some to board other trains that would take them into the city, others to get a taxi. Time for some was paramount, others calmly sat it out. It was some time before the ambulance crew attended, the rush hour making road travel difficult, but the patient was now stabilized, resulting in a quick transfer to the platform and the waiting ambulance. We had been delayed by more than half an hour, but I like to think the same would be done for me should I ever have need!

What follows is an incident that really should not have happened, one that was to lead to hospitalisation for one young women and legal prosecution. The incident came about when I was working a twelve car train up to Tonbridge from Hastings. Prior to leaving Hastings passengers for certain stations were informed not to travel in the rear six carriages as normal procedure, due in part to restricted platform lengths and tunnels. I had even walked through the rear six carriages informing passengers that they needed to move to the front six carriages at Royal Tunbridge Wells if they wanted High Brooms. One particular young couple were more engrossed in themselves than listening to me, but I gave them the benefit of the doubt and left them to it. We arrived in Royal Tunbridge wells and I noticed the young lad get off, his girlfriend remained on the train. I had not actually checked tickets, time did not allow, so I assumed the young women was going on to Tonbridge. Well we pulled into High Brooms and just a few passengers left the train. As we pulled away from the platform and had picked up some speed I suddenly saw a door flung open and the young women jump from the train. As she landed on the platform, her feet together and facing in the direction of travel, the momentum spun her round and she went crashing to the ground flat on her back. I had no option but to signal the driver to stop. The train ground to a halt, the engine many meters along the track, my guards brake barely on the platform. As I ran back along the platform I feared the worse. The young women lay completely still, her eyes closed. Kneeling down beside her I looked for signs of life and was greatly relieved when I saw that she was breathing. There was no blood, but she was unconscious and completely out of it. By now the driver was showing concern and another passenger had joined me. The station was unstaffed, so no help there. We made the casualty as comfortable as possible by covering her in a coat and padding her head before I had a quick word with the driver and then called for an ambulance using the phone on the platform. Time seemed to take forever before the ambulance turned up, but in reality they were pretty quick. Between caring for the casualty, liaising with the driver and the emergency services, I had to pacify the passengers and attempt to ascertain some information regarding the identity and details of the young women. Being on the main line and in a station meant we were safe from other trains, so at least that was not a concern. As usual in such cases, the ambulance crew were most efficient and we were able to proceed on our way after some twenty five minutes or so. Obviously this caused a delay on all the services following as we were blocking the permanent way. Upon arrival in Tonbridge I reported to the supervisor, but was rather reluctant to say much on account of covering for another guard. I was in fact partaking in a recognised bit of duty swopping where the Tonbridge guard worked my train up to Tonbridge so as to get off duty earlier, with me working his later train. No risk to the public resulted from this, we were all qualified guards, but it meant that the identity of the guard was in question if an incident happened such as this. The supervisor sent me on my way with no words of recrimination, instructing me to file a full report with my supervisor in Hastings.

I returned to Hastings fearing the worse, disciplinary action at the least. My report duly filed I awaited the flack, but none came. Presumably my reactions at the time of the incident, and the fact that I carried out my duties as a guard were to stand in my favour, after all, I had not simply closed my brake van window and returned to the paper, which was the wont of many a guard. It was only some time later that I was told of the fate of the young woman. She had to be hospitalised due to concussion, but had not suffered any long lasting effects and was now well. But the outcome for her was not good as BR was obliged to prosecute her for jumping from a moving train against the regulations, thereby putting her life and others at risk. Lessons were learned from this incident, the hard way, but at least she lived to tell the tale. As for me and the other guards who regularly swopped duties, we thought long and hard before continuing the practice, supervisors too in allowing it.

My next couple of incidents involved some of the people I worked alongside, not involving me directly 'but by the grace of God go I' as they say. First was a serious incident that took place at Charing Cross. As previously mentioned, one of our duties involved working a commuter train up to Cannon Street then back across the Thames and round to Charing Cross, empty, so as to provide a return public service down to Hastings. Official practise required the guard to travel in the brake-van located either at the rear of the train, or in the middle, depending on its makeup. Often as not though, the guard would travel up front with the driver so as to take in the view of the river. The one problem with this was that you might be held up by signals going through Waterloo East, making it difficult to stop passengers from boarding the train. Well on this occasion all seemed to be going well until the approach into Charing Cross. For some reason the driver failed to bring the train to a halt and went on to hit the buffers. Ordinarily this should have stopped the train, but presumably the speed was just too much along with the weight and momentum. The outcome was that the engine sheared off its boggy and came to a halt some way onto the concourse of the station! I believe no one was killed, but some members of the public received injuries from flying bits of barrier and debris. It's a wonder no one was killed. The inquiry went on for some time, as did the repairs to the station. I never did hear the full outcome, and haven't been able to find a copy of the report; rumour was rife, as was the case when such incidents happened.

The other incident took place on the Hastings to Ashford line, again involving a train being run as empty coaching stock and the guard travelling up front with the driver. It was March 1980 and the train was approaching Appledore Station on the up-line, heading for Ashford, when it left the rails and landed on its side. The enquiry came to the conclusion excessive speed was the cause of the accident, basically driver error. The driver, a well-liked colleague, was to lose his life. The guard escaped with minor injuries, inadequate route knowledge being sighted for his actions. The whole depot was shocked by this incident and, along with the previous one, made you think about what really was the cause. Did travelling with the driver contribute to the accidents? Was the distraction actually the cause?

Now comes three more incidents, all resulting in fatalities, and all that involved the train I was working one way or another. The first happened again on the Hastings to Ashford line. We had just pulled into Hastings Station when were informed that our train had been the cause of a fatality at Rye. Both I and my driver looked blankly at each other, not really knowing how we were to blame, or believing that we were. It was some time before we got to hear the full story. We had just pulled out of Rye Station when the up-train pulled in, utilising the double line at this point which allowed the two services to pass on what was otherwise a single track. Unfortunately, a pedestrian had attempted to cross the tracks, via the footpath crossing just south of the station, as we passed. She had stepped out from behind our train into the direct path of the incoming service. She had not heard the other train and was just too slow. This was a terrible loss of a life, it should not have happened. I can remember seeing this woman, along with a few other people, waiting to cross the tracks. My driver had sounded the engine's horn and they had stood off, but little did we know what was to come. How sad. I find it hard to understand just how the driver of the up-train felt seeing her in front of him and not being able to do anything. All too often this is the way of it where trains are concerned.

My next two recollections take place on the Hastings to Tonbridge line, both in or around Wadhurst. In much the same way as the incident above, we were informed upon arrival in Hastings that our train had been involved in the death of a woman. A body had been discovered, I believe by track maintenance staff, in one of the tunnels south of Royal Tunbridge Wells. The timing pointed to either our train, or that of the up-train, as being the one that hit her as we had passed in the tunnel. Due to the nature of the incident, an inquest was established to seek a cause of death. Amongst others, I was called as a witness to give evidence. Truth be told, I knew absolutely nothing. I referred to my log book for any information that might help recall the incident. I had noticed a loud knocking noise at one point whilst travelling through the tunnel and had checked the carriage adjacent to the brake-van for an open door. All seemed well, so I had no cause to worry. Such noises were fairly common, especially when passing another train in a tunnel. This left the inquest in somewhat of a quandary, had the woman jumped, fallen or been pushed from my train or the other, or had she actually entered the tunnel on foot? We shall never know for sure, but I believe foul play was ruled out.

In bringing this rather sad chapter to an end I'll relate one last incident that whilst macabre is, all the same, a little amusing in its odd sort of way. We had arrived at Wadhurst Station, working a passenger train down to Hastings from London. Here we were stopped for some time whilst information was made available to us. A train had pulled into a London terminal station with a human head caught up in the underside of the leading engine's couplings! This had obviously caused a stir and had to be dealt with as soon as possible. Was this a case of someone being hit and decapitated by a passing train? Was there a headless corpse lying on the tracks somewhere, and if so, where? Timings and other leads were quickly looked at, the outcome being that all tunnels needed to be searched. This is where we came in. Although it was known that at least two other services had previously passed through the tunnel at Wadhurst, in both directions, ours was the first since the information had come to light. We were now being asked to proceed at a walking pace in order to search for any corpse that might lay on the tracks. In order to achieve this, I was to travel up front with the driver and use my hand-lamp in an effort to view the track ahead. The passengers were kept in ignorance of what we were about to do as we set off into the darkness. Quite what was expected of us if we had found a headless corpse, I don't know, that's assuming neither of us feinted! Needless to say we found nothing, much to our relief. We never did get to hear the end to this incident, but I'll never forget being asked to undertake that search.

Terrorism.

During the 1970's and 80's, terrorism was a fact of life (not much has changed there), the IRA upping the ante by bringing their activities to the UK mainland. The railways were a particular soft target, especially the mainline commuter stations in London. By causing fear and disruption in the capital, the whole country was put on high alert and the government made to look ineffective. These were troubled times, made the more difficult when the use of litterbin-bombs were introduced alongside letter-bombs and unattended parcel-bombs. No matter how many times warnings were given and it was stressed that people should not leave parcels, bags or cases, unattended, they did!

It was the main terminal stations that were the worst affected although stations such as London Bridge and Waterloo were to be targeted too. Some actually became the location for explosions with the associated injuries to staff and the travelling public that inevitably resulted. Charing Cross, Waterloo along with Cannon Street stations were of primary concern to me, these being places my work took me to and had to spend extended time in. I was fully aware of the risks to myself and the passengers as the trains emptied out, providing opportunity for maximum damage, using the minimum of explosives. Just one successful bomb brought huge gains for the IRA, the disruption and chaos ensuing could not only inflict a crippling close down of the working heart of the City of London, but the knock on effect sent shock waves throughout the country. With just a couple of small litterbin explosive devices proving successful, the merest hint of an attack could lead to a false alarm, something the IRA, and the odd nutter, capitalised on, with hoaxes proving legion. Alerts came thick and fast, with vigilance being maintained to the point that everyone was watching everyone else. This state of affairs led to precautions being taken, areas being closed off whilst checks were being made, trains halted both in and out of stations, mail boxes being sealed up and litter bins removed. It was not uncommon to find cinemas and theatres having to be cleared, with performances halted. The disruption both to ordinary life and in the workplace could be quite major, but during all this time I never once remember panic taking over. It's the direct effects on the latter, my workplace, that I'll now address.

With false alarms, let alone the real thing, train schedules could be put into disarray. It became common to be stopped for long periods of time prior to being allowed to enter the main terminal stations. This of course caused upheaval, frustration and anger amongst the passengers, but not directed at BR or ourselves as I recall. To a great extent there was a form of solidarity amongst the travelling public and rail staff, a feeling of we were all in it together and just had to get on with it. Some people acquainted it to the so called 'blitz spirit' that had prevailed during WW11, but as I'm not old enough to know how that felt, I can't really say. I do know, however, that such delays could cause consternation and sometimes fear. A single incident will do to illustrate this. We had arrived just south of the river and were making slow time towards Cannon Street station. Obviously some alert was going on causing queuing of services waiting to disgorge their passengers. We were finally brought to a stop short of the station, out over the Thames. I was not at all happy about this as surely to goodness we were now just sitting targets? My reasoning went along the lines that a hoax call could prompt an alert in the station, whilst a bomb set under the bridges that carried the rail tracks could cause untold death and destruction. Perhaps my imagination was doing overtime, or I was allowing the situation to get to me, whatever way you look at it though we were in a vulnerable location. It was this incident that really brought home to me the seriousness of the situation, we were but pawns in a fight that none could win and only diplomacy and negotiation would solve.

Following on from such delays were the ever present finding of an unattended package, case or other piece of luggage. This happened all too often, but generally the owner was located or returned to claim their forgotten item. As a guard I had been trained to look out for such articles, to go methodically through a train checking for such unattended items, specifically when a train arrived at a terminus station. Should you come across such a piece, then the carriage had to be cleared if in transit, but if in a station, then the train along with the platform. The precautions caused untold upheaval and involved not only BR staff but the police, bomb disposal squads and other emergency services on occasion. It was upon arrival in Cannon Street station that such an incident happened to me. Going through the train, expecting to find no more than a newspaper, I was suddenly confronted with a parcel wrapped in brown paper tied with string. Initially thoughts of all kinds raced through my brain, but as the train was now virtually empty of passengers my immediate fear of people being killed or injured subsided. My driver was by now making his way to the rear of the train in order that we work it empty back to Charing Cross in preparation to form a return service down to Hastings. I caught his attention and explained the dilemma. Knowing that in all probability this was a harmless parcel, and that if we wanted to get home that day, our best bet was to remove it and get out of there. My driver was not so sure but agreed to continue to the rear of the train where he should be safe. Meanwhile I checked the rest of the train for any passengers and went to have a word with the platform staff. Having explained the situation they were unsure as to what to do, no one wanting to make a decision. I returned to the parcel, expecting a frantic passenger to turn up at any moment to reclaim it. No one appeared, so with time to our departure drawing near I re-entered the carriage, carefully picked up the parcel and took it out onto the platform. I then carried the parcel along the platform to where it started to go out over the Thames. Once there I placed the parcel gently on a bench and returned down the platform. No one had made any decision at this point as to what to do, so I checked the starter signal was in our favour and said in that case we'd be off. Informed of the location of the parcel and its description, I calmly turned around and got into my brake-van and gave the driver the signal to go, leaving the problem with the Cannon Street staff! My log book that day duly recorded the facts, but as our duties had not been delayed I did not feel inclined to fill in a report, nor was one ever asked for. Based on the fact that I was not quizzed over this incident, or that I heard no report of major disruptions, I can only assume the parcel was just that and that the owner turned up and all was sorted.

Of course such precautions were not fool proof against bombs and they did on occasion go off. I more than once saw the after effects of bombs, the burnt and singed litterbins, building surfaces and cordoned off areas an ever present reminder that vigilance was required. But the presence of the threat was more potent than the threat itself. Luckily for the general public at large, the IRA did not seem to have the capacity, or available explosives, to mount a sustained and truly devastating campaign. Whether that was down to the security services is debatable, more likely a realisation by the IRA themselves that such a course of action would only make their cause seem utterly alien to all.

Testing times.

Being a guard meant just that, you were responsible for the safety of those travelling on your train. That included everyone, so when, or if, you became aware of a danger that might directly affect those travelling, it was your duty to avert that danger, or at the least get people out of harm's way. A common form of danger, or perceived danger, is one of unruly groups of individuals running amuck. Often such people were young men, sometimes drunk, but nearly always abusive and loud. The real problem here was containing them and preventing them from harming not only other passengers, but themselves too.

Whilst returning from Charing Cross on a service down to Hastings I was suddenly aware of a passenger knocking on my brake van door. The passenger turned out to be an off duty BR staff member. He informed me that a group of youngsters were causing mayhem and intimidating other passengers. Apparently a fire extinguisher had also been set off. Together we went through the train to ascertain the full problem. We came across a few small groups of youths, both males and females, being rather loud, obviously fuelled up on alcohol, but not outright hostile. Further investigation revealed a missing fire extinguisher and the resultant mess from it having been set off within the confines of the lobby between carriages. With no sign of the extinguisher and an open nearside window, I concluded it had been thrown from the train. Questioning a few passengers who appeared rather cowered, it transpired my thoughts were right and that the culprits were elsewhere on the train. With the assistance of the off duty staff member, we searched the rest of the train and assessed the situation, a few further groups of youths being located along with a couple of locked toilet doors. It was obvious that action would have to be taken to contain the situation and notify the control centre that there was a possible obstruction on the line, i.e. the fire extinguisher. Accessing another brake van I called up the driver on the intercom and asked him to stop at the next available signal with a phone in order to relay a message to the control centre. Our next official stop was Orpington, a little over ten minutes away, so the two of us returned through the train in order to put a stop to any further anti-social behaviour.

I had decided to round up the various youths and 'corral' them in the buffet car, the bar being closed and shuttered. It proved surprisingly easy to move them through the train, to the point that I was directing them to go ahead of us and wait in the buffet car, which they duly did. Whether it was the size of my new found companion, my uniform or the manner in which I related to them, I'm not sure, but they complied with little or no argument. We also managed to get a couple of youths out of the toilets where we found evidence of drug usage, exactly what I was expecting. As this was being done, the driver had slowed to a halt and relayed my message then slowly moved off again, hardly anyone realising we had stopped. By the time we had got all the youths in the buffet car, apart from perhaps two still holding out in a toilet, we pulled into Orpington station. There on the platform was a reception committee, several police officers, some with dogs. The youths were somewhat taken aback by this, me too for that matter. I hadn't expected such a show of force, let alone the dogs! No one was allowed to leave the train at first, the police boarding at various points. With both male and female officers aboard a search was carried out of each and every youth for drugs, drink and any weapons. Well several of the former were found, but no weapons to my knowledge. Some drugs along with associated needles were found down the pans in the toilets, the last two youths also being extracted when they realised they were trapped. Those that had drugs on them, along with those youths from the toilet, were hauled off with the remainder once again confined to the buffet car. By now we had been held up around twenty minutes. A small police presence travelled with us on to Sevenoaks where again we were met by a heavy police presence. A few of the youths left the train here. With each further station down to Royal Tunbridge Wells a similar picture unfolded until all the youths had finally left the train.

This was the one and only time I can remember such a large police turnout, the dogs adding another dimension! I can only think that the police had previous knowledge that something was afoot, or it was pure coincidence that they had both the numbers of officers and dogs in one place at such short notice. Again, as with other incidents, I got no follow-up information about the outcome, or the fire extinguisher for that matter!

Another incident comes to mind that was to test my abilities as a guard. Again, travelling down to Hastings from London, but this time no belligerent youths were involved, merely a wayward driver! We had left Royal Tunbridge Wells and were going along quite nicely, keeping good time when we entered Wadhurst Tunnel. I was in the brake van checking my log book as slowly I became aware that we seemed to be taking far longer than usual in passing through the tunnel. Getting to my feet I looked out of the window, something wasn't quite right. It was only when I dropped the window that I realised we were in fact stationary, putting my hand out to touch the wall confirmed it. The engines were working as if we should be moving, the train was vibrating and the noise was what you'd expect, but we were stationary? Looking along the train I could see a tiny light at the end of the tunnel, daylight, which meant we were some way from the exit. My obvious reaction was to get on the intercom to the driver, but the noise, along with the poor performance of the technology, prevented me from getting any audible response.

Rather perplexed, I set off through the train to check all was OK. Some of the passengers were aware that something was wrong so I calmed their fears and said that all was well. Getting to the forward brake van I had a dilemma, the recently blocked off doors to the engine rooms meant I could not access the driver's cab directly. I could either try the intercom again, or get down onto the track and make a dash to the driver's cab. There really was no choice as the train was still stationary and the engines revving. It was the tracks for me. Dropping to the trackside I promptly moved as rapidly as I could alongside the ballast within the confines of the tunnel to the far end of the engine, using my hand-lamp for light and some reassurance. Once at the steps to the cab I climbed up and held tight to the hand rails whilst at the same time leaning across to the open driver's window.

With my head close up to the window I looked into the cab, fearful of what I might find. There sat the driver, his hand on the regulator, his head facing straight ahead, but his eyes were closed! I reached into the cab and shook his arm. That did the trick, he suddenly tensed bolt upright. As if in a dream he turned to me with a look of shock and disbelief on his face. With my presence now confirmed, I opened the engine room door and went through into the cab, closing the inner door behind me. Half dazed the driver gave me a strange look as I sat down beside him. There was a difficult silence, only broken when I made to speak but he opened first. I can't quote his words, but he was obviously both shocked and annoyed that the situation had come to this. I listened quietly, after all, whatever had transpired, he was the driver and the only one able to get us out of this tunnel. It was the old chestnut along the line of leaves on the track causing the wheels to slip and spin. Sure enough the wheels had been slipping, probably spinning too judging by the noise, smoke and smell, but he had instantly let the regulator rise upon my appearance which allowed the engines to return to just ticking over. Now fully awake and aware, the driver very slowly opened the regulator again, feeling the traction as we moved forward. But the damage had been done as his actions had made hollows in the rails and worn the rims of the wheels causing what is known as flat tyres! Assured that he was now back in control I returned along the track and re-joined the train, before we proceeded on out of the tunnel and into Wadhurst Station. As we moved slowly towards the station you could hear the noise as the wheels dropped in turn into the hollows in the rails; the feeling as the carriages went over the hollows was something else. By now we had lost some time, also my confidence was somewhat shaken, but I had to give the driver the benefit of the doubt, so kept quiet about what I had seen. This was a case of putting it down to experience and just hoping that you hadn't let something pass that would come back and bite you in the arse! The remainder of our journey was undertaken at reduced speed, the effected rails, and wheels, having to be attended to later.

To round off this chapter I'll quickly relate an occurrence that was to make the hairs stand up on the back of my neck. It was probably around November time and I was working the Hastings to Ashford service. The weather was quite mild, but damp and, in places, foggy. Having left Ore, Guestling Green and Three Oaks behind we came out onto the flat marshland that lies around Winchelsea and Rye. Here we began to hit fog, not the odd bit, but dense banks of fog, the sort you can't see your hand when held out in front of you. This was not good as it meant reducing speed so as not to overshoot a signal. Well it became so bad that the driver was reluctant to continue without further precautions. Under the circumstances our best course of action was for me to travel up front with the driver so as to provide another pair of eyes. It was uncanny, you thought you knew the line like the back of your hand, but in these conditions all your senses were useless; quite literally sound, distance and speed were baffled, fogged you might say! You knew that a signal was due, but for the life of you it came as a surprise when you saw it. It wasn't just the chance of missing a signal that was making us so cautious, but the possibility of not seeing someone using one of the footpath crossings. This was not something either of us had experienced before and didn't wish to again.

Them and us!

You might think that the title of this chapter refers to the situation that is commonly believed to have prevailed between management and workers, and to a certain extent you'd be right. There has always, or so it seems, been this perceived divide, a kind of unwritten war of attrition. Much of this has been fostered and stirred up over the years by the media, the unions, governments and even management themselves. It's seen as a way of forcing through change, a bargaining tool, a way of exerting pressure from both sides. But such an outlook is both confrontational and serves no positive purpose in that it blinkers both sides to good working practises and creates barriers that needn't exist. I do not intend to push any political point of view here, merely express my own observations on how such a system affected me personally, both in my work and relationships with fellow workers.

As stated earlier, upon entering service with BR it was a legal requirement at the time that I belong to a union. I do not fully understand, or appreciate, how we got to this position, or if it purely related to public sector services. What mattered to me was that the system in place should aid better working practises, safety, proficiency, and be fair to all concerned. The country had gone through a lot of political turmoil in the previous decade, with union and government relations being at rock bottom, or so it seemed to me. Tensions were running high, transport services, particularly the train drivers union ASLEF were becoming more confrontational with strike action being resorted to all too often. This type of power struggle went to the heart of the unions and management, the government seemingly powerless to stop it, or dragging their feet purposefully, I don't know which, but involving all whether they wished or not. I felt very angry that I had no say in what was happening, or rather, my voice didn't seem to count. We were told by our union to go out on strike, initially the odd day or so was official action. The rail system was effectively shut down, management running an emergency service, but stations and depots closed to all. There was no question of being given the opportunity to go into work and show your disagreement with how things were being handled. As time dragged on and funds started to dry up, the union implemented selected unofficial strike action with us guards being expected to withhold out labour, but with no strike pay or a solution being found. I for one was not happy. I could not afford to go without pay, besides I felt this should all be sorted out around the negotiating table. It was quite clear to me that we were being used as pawns in a game that none could win and only those in high positions of power might benefit from.

It was at this time I was forced into non-cooperation with my union. Management had sensed the change of mood and opened up the workplace once more to those who wished to return to work, resulting in a skeleton service initially. Some, like me, went into work, running the gauntlet of fellow guards and drivers who were in it to the bitter end. I felt compelled into making a stand, in turn being branded a 'black leg', 'scab' and far worse by some. These were not happy times, the strike action slowly coming to an end with both workers and management being further divided, but not just that, workers in all sectors now finding themselves pitted against their fellow workers. Well, as is the way in such things, time healed the rift superficially and things slowly returned to normal. Working practises, wage structures and other areas of contention were addressed, not to everyone's satisfaction, but then that will never be the case. This then had been the second time that unions had had a direct bearing on my life and work. Having been in management in my previous career I fully appreciated the problems in arriving at a balanced and fair regime, such working is never easy to achieve, but you have to try. The experience had not changed my view that such organisations were any longer relevant in this day and age and in fact it had only reinforced it.

Union representation when negotiating changing work practises or sorting out an individual's problem should be open to all if they wished, well that was my belief, with such membership also up to the individual. This was not the case during my employment with BR, leading not only to enforcement of union rules and wants, but resentment and frustration on my part that my hands were tied. With the changes came improved working practises, so the management would have you believe, new technology and better trains for the public, but not always joined up thinking! A good case of this is given now. The Hastings to Ashford line had suffered from lack of investment, due in part to low passenger numbers, but old working practises and even older rolling stock and crossings that led to a chicken and egg type situation. Part of the temporary solution was to make the line single track in places, to close halts and generally downgrade the service. But then come's a review, a revival of fortunes when it's announced that new working stock is to be introduced; this all sounds very positive until you learn the nitty gritty of it. The new open units were to have automatic doors and incorporate public announcement systems. The guard was now to act as a conductor, walking through the train collecting fares and answering any questions the public might have. All seemed bright, friendly and modern, just the answer to the old fashioned units where formerly carriages were isolated from one another, some indeed still having individual compartments! Plans were put in place to introduce the new units to us, the guards, with the drivers being trained up first.

Following the drivers' training, concerns were voiced about the safety of passengers when alighting and boarding, the doors being operated by the driver who would not be able to see all parts of the train. Another factor was just how you went about isolating a carriage in the event of a fire or other need. The training didn't seem to address these issues, but then at this moment we as guards had not received any training, so all was conjecture. I, like my fellow guards, waited for the notice when training would take place. Initially no notice came and the first we knew of the new unit was when we were confronted with it in the depot. A short notice basically stated we were to familiarise ourselves with it. In effect this meant we had little or no experience of the new public address system, what, if anything, was different when testing the braking system and how you went about isolating a carriage. Being faced with this dilemma I promptly requested that training be given prior to working the new units. Management replied by arranging for an instructor to provide a short training session in the use of the new public address system and the units. A few days later found a small group of us guards being addressed by an instructor. He paid particular attention to the public address system and the changes within the unit's layout along with the automatic door. When we started looking around the exterior it soon became obvious that this 'instructor' had little or no knowledge concerning the braking systems or how to isolate the carriages. By now I was somewhat annoyed, as it was clear that we were being hoodwinked, or put more bluntly, taken for a ride! Squaring up to the 'instructor' I asked him directly what training he had received himself on these units. At this point he had to admit to only having been given the minimum of training by one of our own drivers earlier that day. With that revelation I simply turned on my heels and walked away, saying that I would only work these units when a qualified 'instructor' was brought in to instruct me.

Following on from this I was asked to explain my actions by both the union rep and management. I duly told them that the reasoning behind my belligerent attitude was that as a guard I was expected to protect my passengers, that required me to know the finer details of how the braking system worked along with how to isolate carriages! No more was said until shortly after another 'instructor' turned up and at last the issues were resolved, but not to my personal satisfaction. Whilst working these new units we as guards were no longer held responsible for the operation and secure closure of the doors. The drivers were now held responsible, which I found not only unfair on them, but from a safety point of view, dubious to say the least. This was one of the issues that led me to review my situation and look at moving on, the tightly proscribed rules and regulations just not proving flexible in an age of new technology and faster trains. As a guard I was now being expected to pay more attention to revenue collection, as staff were being reduced at stations and some were becoming unmanned. This state of affairs didn't bode well, health and safety regulations were being compromised so I thought, and still do. As an example of just how difficult things had become, I'll relate one final incident that explains how I came to give my notice and extricate myself from what, at the time, I came to see as a Nationalised calamity, but on reflection now see that almost any large business suffers from the same problems.

Royal Tunbridge Wells station on a fairly quiet duty. I had gone through the train checking tickets earlier, so had noted three lads get on at Frant, but had not had the time to check theirs. Aware these lads probably didn't have tickets, I positioned myself alongside the ticket collector at the exit from the platform to see. Sure enough, one lad played innocent when stopped and asked for his ticket, another pushed past and the two of them ran off, the third, seeing he couldn't get past us ran back along the platform and made to climb the wall. I was quick on his heels as he mounted a seat and was hauling himself to the top of the wall. Reaching up I grabbed the back of his coat and pulled him back onto the platform. 'The game up' as they say, he came quietly. Walking back to the exit gate we were met by the Station Master and ticket collector. A quick exchange of words and it was soon established the lads had got on the train at Frant without making any attempt to purchase tickets. The plan was to mingle with other passengers upon exiting the station and avoid payment. Well two had succeeded whilst the third was now looking rather sorry for him-self, and was left having to carry the can. What followed was to prove not only unexpected, but left me feeling side-stepped and undervalued at the time. The Station Master addressed the lad who was around sixteen or seventeen in a robust fashion shall we say. He ripped him off a strip before finishing by telling him to "fuck off and don't let me catch you again"! I was not at all impressed by this, it left the matter unresolved and as I saw it, the lad getting away with revenue evasion, the very thing we as guards were being pushed to enforce. With no authority to override the Station Master, and little time in which to remonstrate with him, the matter had to finish there. I returned to my train, frustrated and angry. In retrospect the Station Master's response probably did have the desired effect, that of putting the fear of god up the lad and making him less likely to try the same thing again; but I still doubt that, the lads no doubt regrouping and thinking how clever they were in getting away without paying. What really annoyed me though, was the way in which the Station Master's action had undermined both mine and the ticket collector's positions. Without showing a united front, there was no way you could implement the rules and regulations, it also left you feeling you could not be sure of getting the desired support and back-up when needed from management.

The above couple of incidents go to highlight my reasons for finally giving my notice and quitting the job. This was in 1982. However, with a family and mortgage to maintain and having chucked in a well-paid job, I had effectively shot myself in the foot; but at the time I could see no other course of action that would avoid me getting into a terrible argument with management and at the same time keep me sane! I was forced to seek unemployment benefit and sign on the dole while I reappraised my situation. That put me in a difficult position in that under the regulations at the time, anyone who gave up a job, and put themselves on the dole, without good reason, had to wait six weeks before any money would be paid to them. This was obviously a deterrent to help avoid shirkers, or spongers, living off the state. With little reserve savings I was forced to borrow money and seek reduced payments on my mortgage. At the same time I appealed to the Department of Employment, requesting that they pay me unemployment benefit straight away on the grounds that I had given notice due to impossible work requirements and poor management. Of course such procedures take time, so things got pretty tight, but the outcome was to vindicate my actions in that unemployment allowance was granted, and back-dated to when I left the service of BR. Likewise, an industrial tribunal found I had had good cause for handing in my notice and awarded me full pension rights and pay for holiday's outstanding and unworked notice time. So came to an end a period in my working life which I had found both fulfilling and worthwhile, but like so many areas in the workplace, fraught with difficulties.

Some good memories.

As with any period of reflection, you can usually find some good memories, times or events that proved both enlightening and funny. So with this in mind I've come up with the following, a collection of isolated stories and odd happenings.

One of the things that stand out in my mind was being late for duty, a rare occurrence for me, and the reason behind it. I've often heard it asked, 'Do you remember where you were the day this or that happened'? The usual one is the assignation of John F. Kennedy in Dallas, Texas, on 22nd November 1963. For me though this means little, being only nine at the time and no doubt having other things on my mind. For my wife however, it being her birthday and some years older, it will always be remembered. More recently was the 7/11 bombings in London. This was on my birthday and I was at home in Kendal at the time and it left me feeling devastated. But good memories do come to mind, the main one being the raising of the Mary Rose. For those of you of a certain age, or with little or no idea of what the hell I'm talking about, this was the day, 11th October 1982, on which the wreck of King Henry V111's flag ship The Mary Rose was winched from the sea bed in The Solent, and finally broke surface after lying below the waves for 434 years! She had sunk during a naval engagement on 19th July 1545 whilst under the command of Sir George Carew, watched from the safety of the shore (amongst others) by Henry V111 and Lady Carew, the vice-admiral's wife. Few survived the sinking, the vice-admiral being one of those that lost their life. Anyway, history lesson over, I'll get back to the event being played out in front of my eyes back in October 1982. Like many other people I was watching live television coverage of the salvage operation. The cradle that had been built specially in order to winch the wreck out of the water had just broken the surface and everyone involved, including most people watching I fancy, let out an almighty cheer. This was ground-breaking stuff. But then came a set-back that put a lump in my throat, part of the cradle snapped and dropped. All looked in jeopardy, the wreck being lost, or crushed at the very least! With my heart all of a flutter, I had to get up from the television screen and go to work as I was already running late and couldn't put it off any longer. With many a backward glance I reluctantly left the house.

Getting to the depot late meant one of two things, either risking not reading the notices and checking the unit over properly so as to make up time, or admitting being late and going through the proper procedures. I have to admit on this occasion to going with the first option, something I'm not too proud of. The benefit of this was that I got my unit out on time and through to Hastings ready to work a passenger service. That allowed me time to drop into the supervisor's office and check on developments concerning the salvage! You can see from this that I have a deep interest in our history and heritage, as surprisingly did many of the staff concerning this particular event. We waited with baited breath whilst the cradle was first checked over and then hoisted clear of the water and the whole eventually brought safely into dock in Portsmouth. The rest they say is history, but a day never to be forgotten from my point of view.

It was my interest in history and archaeology that led me into taking a BSc Hons degree in Heritage Conservation as a mature student later in life, but for now, as that's another story, I'll tell of a few related incidents. Other members of staff soon got to know of my interest and knowledge concerning ancient artefacts, stamps, coins and the like, so periodically I'd be presented with something to identify. A train driver once brought me a coin to look at. It was a rather nice bronze of the Roman emperor Hadrian; a large sestertius if I remember rightly, dating to around 118AD. When I asked him where he had got it from, his reply was that it had come out of his elderly mother's button box! How it got there we'll never know.

As mentioned before, spare duty involved often having to spend several hours sitting around the guards' room in the depot, so having something to while away the time was a good idea. On several occasions I took in parts of my various collections for further sorting and research. It was whilst going through assorted loose leaves of my stamp albums that Hastings Station Master paid an unannounced visit. He suddenly appeared, along with another member of management I didn't recognise, to find me engrossed in my research, the table littered with pages of stamps. His immediate reaction was to query just how long it would take me to clear the lot away and be ready to go out on a job? My reply was along the lines of about as long as it would take for any other guard to put his newspaper, pools or playing cards away! There was just no answer to that, so he had to concede that I wasn't delaying readiness for duty, he even went on to show interest in what I was researching,

Hobbies, and other interests as I said, were paramount to getting through a spare duty. Another thing I did was to work on the latest needlepoint I had on the go. Yes you read it right, needlepoint. I got involved initially when my wife asked me to design pictures for her to do in needlepoint. This meant transferring a design, usually taken from one of my photographs, to the canvas using coloured felt tip pens as often as not. Well this led onto making frames for stretching the canvas whilst working and eventually to me working the canvasses. Initially canvasses were made for special events for family and friends, but paid commissions soon followed which prompted us to think about setting up our own craft business and seeking 'the good life', which incidentally was a very popular TV series at the time. So, my work colleagues got used to seeing me beavering away with cottons, woollen yarn and silks as they booked on and off duty! A few even began to bring in similar things to do, no longer feeling inhibited. I certainly wasn't the only member of staff to practise my hobby at work. One of the Hastings supervisors was a keen Gilbert & Sullivan operatic group member and would happily go through his routines, singing to a small audience in his office when time permitted. It was a good break to spend a few minutes between trains listening to a bit of culture, something that I remember with pleasure. Another guard at the depot was into everything concerning steam, engines of all sorts. He'd go to the various steam rallies, Stourpaine in Dorset being his favourite. It was not uncommon to see him poring over the latest associated magazine. Likewise, a Hastings shunter collected and rebuilt early Volkswagen and Porsche cars, particularly

Beetles and those with a bit of history. The range of interests amongst the staff was wide and never ceased to amaze me.

Whilst working a train up to Tonbridge early one morning I noticed several old black and white postcards lying alongside the tracks as we pulled slowly out of West St. Leonard's station. What they were, and how they had got there, I didn't know, but I felt compelled to rescue them. The end of my duty that day actually finished at West St. Leonards with the walk back to the depot. With this in mind, and the day having been dry, I made a point of walking out to the far end of the platform, the postcards being some metres further along the tracks. Putting my high visibility vest on, I hastily walked out alongside the track, picking up the postcards as I went. Having collected around a dozen postcards I returned to the platform. When back at the depot I took the time to look through what I had found. Most were early twentieth century views of Roman remains in Italy, a few, fortified medieval towns in France while the remainder depicted the ruins of Ypres following the carnage of the Battle of the Somme. Someone had obviously thrown them away, but why? Anyway, their loss was my gain, as they now form the basis of my vintage postcard collection.

Collecting and hobbies was the reason behind the next little tale. This concerns the lead up to one Christmas when I was on the lookout for a spinning wheel for my wife. We had become more involved in arts and crafts, hand-spinning and weaving proving the main draw. It was during a break in

Royal Tunbridge Wells that I came across just the wheel, but the cost and getting it home had to be considered. Well I bit the bullet and put a deposit on it so as to have it put by until I was ready to take it away. At the end of the week I returned to the shop in The Pantiles, cash in hand and eager to try it out. Returning from my break with a spinning wheel balanced on my arm raised a few eyebrows, especially when I sat down in the staff room and began to treadle the thing! When my next service to be worked arrived, I calmly carried the wheel into the brake van much to the interest of the guard I was relieving. Working the service up to London and back down to Hastings provided plenty of time in which to get to know the workings of the new wheel and perfect the treadle action. As to quite how I got the wheel home from Hastings station, I can't remember, but it no doubt turned on the goodwill of the Station Supervisor looking after it whilst I returned to the depot and got my car. Needless to say, my wife was made up with her present.

New Year celebrations for me, during the time I was a guard, had to be put on hold. My rostered duty meant that I had to work the last train down from Tonbridge to Hastings New Year's Eve, not arriving in Hastings until nearer one in the morning and getting home finally around half-past if lucky. Although this proved unsociable on occasion, it did mean that I got Christmas off, which was more important to me having young children. Getting someone to change duties was nigh-on impossible, so I settled for what I considered a compromise that held its own little comfort. Depending on weather conditions, and the late night revellers, we'd normally get into Hastings up to ten minutes earlier than scheduled New Year's Eve, everyone wanting to get off home as soon as they could, that included most travellers. This slight change in timing usually meant that at midnight we'd have just left Battle, or Crowhurst. It was at this point, all alone, that I saw in the New Year. It was the only time on duty that I broke a major rule, to imbibe a drop of alcohol! The alcohol concerned was whisky, carried in a small leather covered glass hip-flask with its plated slide on cup. I'd take about half the contents, the equivalent of a single measure; it brought a smile to my face as I looked out across the countryside down Combe Haven to the sea.

Another little incident brings a smile to my face when I think of it. Whilst working a passenger train up to London I walked through to check doors were closed and any passengers who had just boarded had valid tickets. It wasn't a commuter service, so passenger numbers were few. The First Class carriage with its individual compartments was virtually empty as usual, but one passenger sat all alone, his head in a newspaper. In passing I got a quick glimpse of the passenger's face through the window of the compartment. He looked at me, then away pretty sharpish, which made me think perhaps he shouldn't be there. But there was something familiar about his face, a nagging thought stayed with me as I continued checking the doors, so I decided to check him out on my way back through the train. Returning, I politely tapped on the compartment window before sliding the door open. The passenger slowly looked up from his paper, his eyes meeting mine. There was a certain look in those eyes, as if to say 'Yes it is me, what are you going to do about it?' My reaction was one of calm, professional proficiency. "May I see your ticket please Sir?" The ticket was duly produced from the inside ticket pocket of the man's three piece suit and offered for inspection. I took the ticket, checked its validity and destination, clipped it and offered it back. "Thank you Sir. We're running to time. Enjoy the rest of your journey". This said I turned and left the compartment sliding the door quietly behind me. The passenger slowly dropped his head and returned to his paper. Neither spoke of what we both knew; he for his interest in seeing my reaction I presume, me in not giving in to popular adulation and infringing on his privacy. Who was this person I hear you ask? Well not the most important of persons, but for me, one of my favourite actors at the time who could leave me in a heap of uncontrollable laughter, Bill Rowbotham, better known to most people as Bill Owen, 'Compo' Semminite in Last of the Summer Wine. That brief encounter made my day, here was a man who could play such a part, who in reality not only scrubbed up well, but spoke with not a twang of a Northern accent.

Such incidents as that above went to make the job not only interesting, but at times fun. Oh, and in case you were wondering, yes, he did have a First Class ticket. This then is a short compilation of my working life as a train guard on British Rail's Southern Region in the early 1980's. The work was varied, as were the public and staff. You'll note that I haven't put any names to the people I've described, apart that is from Bill Owen, I've avoided this so as to protect those people, and quite possibly myself!

Clive Bowd. Kendal, December 2015.

Printed in Poland
by Amazon Fulfillment
Poland Sp. z o.o., Wrocław